Save Money On
A
Low Income

By
Michael Kaltenbrunner

<Save Money on a Low Income>

The information provided herein is stated to be truthful and consistent, in that any liability, in terms of inattention or otherwise, by any usage or abuse of any policies, processes, or directions contained within is the solitary and utter responsibility of the recipient reader. Under no circumstances will any legal responsibility or blame be held against the publisher for any reparation, damages, or monetary loss due to the information herein, either directly or indirectly.

Respective authors own all copyrights not held by the publisher.

The information herein is offered for informational purposes solely, and is universal as so. The presentation of the information is without contract or any type of guarantee assurance.

The trademarks that are used are without any consent, and the publication of the trademark is without permission or backing by the trademark owner. All trademarks and brands within this book are for clarifying purposes only and are the owned by the owners themselves, not affiliated with this document.

<Save Money on a Low Income>

Table of Contents

<Save Money on a Low Income>

INTRODUCTION

One the most important parts of saving money on a low income is being creative. There are lots of ways to reduce your spending, but many of them are unknown to the average person.

You don't need to be an accountant to learn how to manage your money better. There are many ways to reduce spending, even if you're already living with minimal expenses. Don't wait until your debt gets the better of you. You can stop living from "hand to mouth" — and start saving today!

Is It Possible to Save When You're on a Low Income?

There are millions of people all over the world living from pay check to pay check. When you are struggling just to pay the bills, and keep the debt collectors off your back, the notion of saving money can seem like a little bit of a joke.

If you are serious about changing your financial situation, maybe you are wondering if there is really any hope. This book will show you that there certainly is hope. With the right ideas, some careful

<Save Money on a Low Income>

planning, and dedication — you can learn how to save money on a low income.

How do you suppose parents manage to send their kids to great schools, when they are only earning minimum wage? They put in the necessary effort, and they learn how to get by without spending a lot. Saving is an integral part of becoming a successful person. If you can find ways to hold onto some of the money that you earn, it will allow you to create a better life for yourself, and your children.

GETTING STARTED

Make a Budget

Do you have a budget? If so, that's great. If not — read this section carefully, and make one for yourself before you read the rest of this book. It will make many of the tips easier to put into action, and stop you from getting confused about your finances.

Sorting out your finances is a lot easier when you have a proper budget. Think of it as your road map to saving money. If you don't know how to get where you want to go, you could spend a lot of time lost in the world of financial hardship. The purpose of a budget is to let you identify where you are spending your money, and how you can reduce costs. It makes the task of singling out bad purchases a lot easier.

Start by writing down your income for each month, after taxes. This should include absolutely everything, such as

<Save Money on a Low Income>

salary, pension, child support, interest, etc.

Next, write down all of your expenses for a month. Include everything, like rent or mortgage payments, gas, food, clothing, entertainment, credit card payments, and utilities. Now take your income and subtract those expenses from it. The remaining figure should be money that you can put into savings. If you are spending more than you earn — make some fast changes to your expenses.

Now you can start to find areas where you could save more money by cutting back. Use the other tips in this book to help with this step. Having a budget will make saving much easier.

After you have a budget, don't just put it in a drawer and forget all about it. Look at it every month, or week, and assess your finances. If you notice that you are spending too much on anything, try to compensate so that you always have surplus money for savings.

Evaluate Home Costs

One of the biggest ongoing costs for most people is housing. Even if you don't have any debts or other significant expenses, getting a place to live can take up a big chuck of your monthly budget. If you are renting, take a look at the percentage of your budget that goes toward paying the landlord. Maybe you would be better off moving somewhere cheaper, even if that means making a few sacrifices.

For people who are paying off a mortgage for their own home, contact the bank and see if it's possible to refinance your loan.

Since it's your home, maybe you could rent out a room and use that money to pay off your mortgage faster. It might also be a way to clear other debts, without needing to find a second job.

Pinpoint Your Biggest Expenses

The first thing you should do when planning your finances, is identify the biggest expenses. Are you spending most of your money on rent? Maybe you could find a cheaper place to live. Is your food bill much higher than average, for the number of people living in your home? If so, there is probably some room for cutting back there.

Make a list of every expense, whether it's ongoing or a one-time thing. Whatever you identify, you need to find a way to make those expenses easier to manage. If you absolutely can't go without a certain item, figure out how to reduce costs in other areas.

Get Out of Debt

Next to unemployment and low income, debt is the biggest enemy to saving money. With people having access to loans and credit cards that they really can't afford, the debt of the nation is slowly rising. One of the best ways to live free of debt is to avoid it in the first place. Of course, that is not an option for many people, who are already stuck with regular repayments.

Before you try to save money, it is best to focus on removing your debt. That way,

<Save Money on a Low Income>

you will not be accumulating interest, and wasting even more money over time. It helps to focus on getting rid of one debt at a time, instead of spreading your finances out too much.

Minimum payments are not going to cut it, unless you want to be paying of your debts forever. If you can afford make larger payments, do so. It will remove the debt faster, and lessen the amount of interest that you're stuck with.

Read all of the fine print for your repayment agreement, and make sure that you understand your options. People often make their debt situation worse by being ignorant, or placing blame on the organizations that loaned them money. Take responsibility for your debt, because no one put a gun to your head when you created it.

Hobbies and Collections

Most people in the world have a collection or hobby that regularly costs them money. If it brings joy and value into your life, then maybe it's worth the price. However, people often get to a point where they're just keeping it up out of habit.

Do you need to buy every commemorative plate that you see, or are you better off selling your collection? Are you using your season pass to the local paintball field, or would that money be better off in your savings account?

If you would rather not give up your collection or hobby, maybe you could cut back on the money that goes toward it. Remember, if something isn't making your life somehow better, it's not worth spending on.

Put Away Your Credit Cards

<Save Money on a Low Income>

Credit cards were never designed to provide the public with more money. They are a wonderful way for big companies to keep people poor. Studies have suggested that the average person spends significantly more when they have a credit card in their pocket. It must be something about the ease of using one, and the fact that it never feels like your own money. Of course, your brain will make that connection when the bill comes. Even ATM cards are a bad idea if you are trying to limit your spending. Ideally, you should just pay for things with cash, and only carry what you absolutely need to use.

If you prefer to have a credit card for emergencies, do yourself a favor and hide it. Try leaving it at the home of a relative, to remove temptation. Maybe they can try to talk some sense into you, since you will have to ask them before you use it.

Avoid Commercial Media

One of the easiest ways to save money is also the most simple. Just turn off the television, or at least make an effort to watch it less. Magazines and newspapers are another big pusher of useless products. When was the last time that you read one that wasn't mostly ads?

You would be amazed at how much commercial media changes how people think and act. All of those advertisements that you have been exposing your brain to, are designed to do one thing: get you to open up your wallet. How often have you blown money on something that you don't need, or really even want, just because it was on TV?

Relax and clear your mind with less television and commercial media. You might even find that you can think more clearly, and focus on getting your finances in order. You can also save money on electricity, or subscription television bills. Change Your Thinking

Little Things Count

Finances are often viewed as a big picture, but the little things are very important. Each step that you can take toward saving money, no matter how tiny, will add up in the end.

Make your lunch at home and take it to work, instead of buying something. If you need to run some errands, try to do them all at once to save on gas. Put your spare change into your savings account. Brew your own coffee instead of buying a cup from the cafe down the street.

When you start to think about the multitude of little things that cost money, it becomes easier to start saving.

Be Diligent

Maybe you already guessed that there were extra ways you could save money. Now that you have a lot more tricks to try out, what else is stopping you? People typically fail to save money because they are not diligent. This is not an overnight thing. It takes concentrated effort, over a length of time, to reach a financial goals. In a year from now, would you like to have a fat savings account, or a faint memory of how you gave up all too easily?

Get Some Professional Help

Are your finances in an absolutely dismal state? If you are struggling to find a way to deal with all of the incoming bills and debt payments — maybe you need to ask a professional for some help. You might even be able to get free advice, depending on your situation. Even if you have to pay a fee for help, it could be worth the money that you will save in the end.

Have a Family Goal

Even if you are doing everything in your power to save money, maybe the rest of your family isn't on board. Have you tried talking to them about your hopes and dreams? Tell your loved ones why you want to save money, and try to get them in on that goal.

When everyone in a household works together, it makes saving a whole lot easier. It will also help you to stay focused, and you can encourage one another along the way. Goals are often more manageable when you work as a team.

<Save Money on a Low Income>

Reduce Your Expenses

Power and Water

On the topic of power, take a look at how much of your budget goes toward electricity and gas. Do you need to keep two refrigerators running all year round? How about leaving the TV on while you head down to the store?

Items that are left on standby also use up an alarming amount of power. Try switching things of at the wall, and see how much difference it can make on your next utility bill.

Water is another resource that people tend to overuse. A short shower is just as effective as a 30 minute one. And how about waiting until you can do a full load of washing up, instead of using water to rinse dishes and utensils one at a time?

Install Energy Saving Light Bulbs

Traditional light bulbs use a lot of power, and they don't tend to last as long as more modern alternatives. You can save around 25% on your lighting costs, just by swapping to CFL light bulbs. If you are able to afford the extra initial cost for LED bulbs, they are an even better option. They're rated to use just 2% of what an incandescent bulb burns up. Think about how much you can save on your power, plus you will not need to buy new bulbs nearly as often.

<Save Money on a Low Income>

Turn Off Your Lights!

This simple tip can reduce your electricity bill by a huge amount. Think about how much power you waste, just by having a single light on while you're at work. Even leaving them turned on when you are not in the room is ridiculous. Whenever you take those two seconds that are required to switch a light off, think about the extra dollars that will wind up in your savings account.

Heating and Cooling

How much money do you spend keeping the climate in your home pleasant? No one is suggesting that you let your family freeze, or sweat it out, but a programmable thermostat might be a good idea.

If you tend to use air conditioning a lot in summer, maybe you could try using a fan instead. If your home is really that hot, get out and go to the beach. There is always a better alternative to spending all of your money on power.

Save on Transportation

One of the best ways to reduce costs is to get rid of your car. Ride a bicycle or walk to where you need to go. You can also take public transport, when you need to go farther. This might not be feasible for people who do a lot of driving, but it's worth considering.

Okay, so most people reading this book will probably want to keep their wheels. How about cutting down on how much you drive? Did you need to waste gas to drive down to the corner store? How about that time you drove down to the park with your dog, instead of just walking there?

Ask Your Credit Card Company to Reduce Your Rates

If you must use credit cards for some reason, maybe you could get a reduction in rates. Take the card and see if there's a phone number on it. If not, find a number on the company's website. Give them a call and ask for a reduction in your rates,

<Save Money on a Low Income>

or you will take your business to another company.

If they refuse to help you, ask to speak to someone else, like their supervisor. Even if you just get a percent or two off your rate that can lead to some great savings.

Smart Shopping Tips

Using Coupons

This is a common money saving tip, but you would be surprised at how many people still don't use coupons. The stores give them out expecting that people will take advantage, so why not do it? Once you get a knack for finding the best coupons, you can save some serious cash. Some places will even let you "double up" with multiple deals on the same times. Make sure that you ask if you can use your discount card from the store too.

A lot of coupons are electronic these days, so get online and try to track them down. You don't have anything to lose, but the savings could be outstanding!

Plan All Shopping

If you really want to save money — you can never buy anything just on a whim. Take a look at your spending, and you might be shocked to see how much of

<Save Money on a Low Income>

your budget is leached into pointless, unplanned purchases.

People love to buy things, because they are programmed to do so in modern society. To combat this careless spending, you need to plan all shopping in advance. Take your budget, which you should have, and refer to it while making your plan. In this way, you can "spend" money on paper, before doing it for real.

When you know how much money is allotted for different expenses, it can make you feel like your income is actually bigger. That's because of all the extra money that you're not spending on random, impulse items.

Meal Planning

You can cut down on the costs of eating by planning your meals. Rather than waiting until it's time for dinner, and then throwing something together, have a planned schedule for meals. On Mondays, you might have spaghetti, while Tuesdays could be Taco night.

When you go shopping, you will know which items you need, and in what quantities. It also helps to reduce waste. It's okay to change your meal plan around from week to week, so that you don't get

<Save Money on a Low Income>

bored. Just make sure that you know what you're going to cook before you go shopping.

Write a Grocery List

Before you go to the grocery store or supermarket for your next food shop — write a list. During the week, write things down as you notice that you need them. Take a look at your list before you head to the store, and assess which things you still need. Once you go through the supermarket doors, remind yourself that you will stick to your list, and only buy things that were planned in advance.

You should also never go food shopping with an empty stomach. Doing so increases the chance that you will buy things that you would otherwise be happy to go without. When people are hungry, they have a tendency to buy a lot more food as well.

Compare Grocery Stores

Going to the grocery store near your house might make sense. After all, it's more convenient since you cut down on travel time, and it requires the least amount of fuel. Maybe there is another store in your area that has better prices on the things you regularly buy. Driving a little farther will cost more, but the savings of going someplace else could be worth it.

Keep your next shopping receipt, and use it to compare the prices at a different store. You might be surprised to learn that you have been spending far too much on your weekly food bill.

Buy in Bulk

Buying items in bulk is a great way to save money. The upfront expense seems huge, but you will spend less over time. Of course, you can't do this unless you have some extra income to spare. That is where the rest of the tips in this book will come in handy, including having a proper budget prepared.

Things that keep for months, or years, can be purchased in large quantities. Store them in your basement or garage, and wait for all of those savings to start taking effect. Eventually, you will find that you don't need to buy a whole lot from the supermarket, because you already have everything in bulk.

Buy Used Items

The thought of getting something brand new might be too much for some people to give up. But if you want to save money, buying used clothes, furniture, electronics, and appliances is one of the most effective methods. A lot of people purchase goods they don't need, and quickly realize they would rather have some of the money back instead. You can benefit from their recklessness, by getting their slightly used goods for way less than retail.

Take a look at classified websites, and monitor Facebook groups that deal with used goods. You would be surprised at some of the bargains you can pick up. Some people even sell big brand items that they have never used.

Customer Reward Programs

Even if you don't shop at a certain store, join up for their customer reward program when given the opportunity. Create an email address for the sole purpose of joining these programs. Use it to sign up for everything that is offered to you. One day, you might need to buy something from one of these businesses. That's when you should check your special email inbox, and see if there are any discounts that you can use. With just a small amount of effort, you can make some big savings over time.

<Save Money on a Low Income>

The next time you're buying something and you're asked to join a free reward club, say "yes please!" Those extra minutes that you spend could make a large difference for your finances.
You Can Resist Spending!

Don't Shop for Fun

Just about everyone loves shopping, and there's no denying that it's enjoyable. People use "retail therapy" to deal with their issues, and to unwind. However, you will no longer be one of those people. You should only go shopping when you actually need something, and when you have planned out your purchases in advance.

This is one of the toughest parts involved with saving money. If it were easy to stop shopping for enjoyment, people would have a lot more in their bank accounts.

Give Up Bad Habits

Many people reading this probably smoke cigarettes, drink alcohol, or maybe even take drugs. From a financial point of view, those things are too expensive for anyone on a low income to afford. And then there are all of the other negative aspects that come along with nasty habits. Don't do it! Save your money instead, and find something more rewarding to do with your time.

Wait 30 Days

Any time you are thinking about making a large purchase, or buying something that you don't really need — use the "30 day rule". The urge to spend money often comes as an impulse, but it quickly passes. Sometimes you will regret purchasing an item before you have even gotten it home.

When you feel the need to spend money on a non-necessity, write it down and wait. After 30 days, if you still want the item, it might be worth the cost. You would be surprised how many times you will forget why you wanted to buy a certain product in the first place.

Don't Eat Out

Going to restaurants, diners, and fast food joints is a great way to spend loads of cash. Think about how much it cost you the last time you ate out with your family. Often, the price of just one meal for a few people is the same as a week's worth of groceries.

If you start to miss going out to dine with friends, why not invite them over for dinner instead? Just about any activity that you do in your home is going to be inexpensive. Ask your friends around, and have a potluck where everyone brings a dish. If the weather is pleasant, why not head out to the yard for an old fashioned cookout? Everyone is sure to have a blast, it will not cost much money, and your friends are likely to invite you to their homes to return the favor. You might even make it a regular thing.

Drink Water

You don't need to guzzle down five or ten dollars' worth of soda and juice every day. How about drinking something that you can practically get for free, right out of your kitchen faucet? That's right — water!

Not only does your body need a certain amount of water every day to function properly, but it is the cheapest choice of beverage in the world. If you want to spend less money on food, have a glass of water before each meal. That will make you feel fuller, and help your body to digest your food. If you don't like regular water from your faucet, try using a filtering jug instead.

Say Goodbye to Convenience Food

Instead of buying pre-packaged meals that come in containers and bags, why don't you try making something healthier? Not only will you be getting less chemicals, salt, and sugar, but you can save a lot of money.

If you had tons of extra cash to throw around, then maybe it would make more sense to buy convenience food. But you wouldn't be reading this book if that were the case. Stop wasting money on microwave meals that taste like cardboard, and never even fill you up. Spend a half hour in the kitchen instead, and you will be surprised at what you can come up with.

Cancel Subscriptions and Memberships

Do you pay for subscriptions and memberships that you don't even use? Giving up your place in a club might be difficult to contemplate, but sometimes it's necessary to let things go, especially when they are not needed. Maybe you are paying to receive a magazine that you don't even read. Why waste the money? Cancel those unwanted subscriptions and put the cash into a savings account instead.

When was the last time you actually went to the gym? It's a great idea to stay healthy, but there is no sense in paying for a membership unless you use it. Even if you don't cancel, maybe the thought of it will be enough to get you working out again.

Save On Entertainment And Other Luxuries

No More Cable TV

You might have guessed that your cable television subscription is not a necessity. One of the first things that a personal financial consultant might tell you, is that the cable has to go. You don't need it, and it's taking up too much of your free time anyway.

There are still loads of things to watch for free, especially if you look online. With the time you save not watching cable TV, you can gain some new skills and try to get a raise, or work at starting an additional income stream.

Don't Spend on Entertainment for Kids

For some reason, people assume that children cost a lot to keep amused. Mostly, they can be entertained for practically no money. Items that are typically considered junk can be turned into all sorts of fun activities for young kids.

Egg cartons and newspaper can provide an afternoon of arts and crafts. All you need is some glue or tape, and there's no limit to the things that can be created. How about making a game out of a ball of tin foil and a basket? That's right, you suddenly have your own basketball game!

Kids mostly just want to spend time with you, so you don't need to have money to keep them happy and busy.

Video Games

Video games used to be strictly for kids, but many adults now enjoy them just as much, if not more. The problem with playing video games as an adult, is that people are generally able to buy more of them. Even if doing so is ruining their finances, gamers will generally make sure that they have plenty of new titles to play.

When you do buy a video game, do your research first. Look at reviews and make

<Save Money on a Low Income>

sure that you only buy titles with lots of replay value, which you are going to enjoy. Don't go for the ones that will take a day or two to complete.

Adventure games and puzzle games are a great choice, because they often take a lot of work to get through. There are also many games for PC that are cheap, or even free.

Visit Your Local Public Library

If you love to read, why borrow some books from the library? That's what they are primarily for, so why not get your reading fix for free? How many times do you actually read a book twice anyway? Maybe you would be better off borrowing it, reading it, returning it — and saving yourself some cash.

You might not realize it, but public libraries are good for more than just books. Many of them also have CDs, DVDs, sporting goods, computer software, and even video games.

Libraries tend to take on the role of community center in some areas too. You might find some free classes, or fun things to do with your children. If you need to use a computer, but don't want to spend money on one, you can also access them at your library.

Make The Most Of What You Have

Learn to Mend Your Own Clothes

These days, when an item of clothing gets torn, what do most people do? They throw it away and head to the store to buy a replacement. What a huge waste of money and goods. If your shirt gets a busted button, find one that matches and sew it back on yourself. When you get a hole in your sock, fix it instead of buying another pair.

Minor repairs are easy to do with just a needle and some thread. In time, you will start to wonder how you ever let yourself be so wasteful in the first place.

Assess What You Own

If you often get the urge to buy new things, try going through what you already own. Maybe you will find some belongings that you could really use, but have forgotten about. This will help to keep you busy when you want to go out and shop too.

Another great idea is to sort out all of your things that you no longer need. Once you have enough items, it is time to have a yard sale and make some extra cash. There's no sense stockpiling a bunch of stuff that you will never use. You can also sell your used goods on eBay and make a killing.

Buy Durable Appliances

When you are strapped for cash, it can be tempting to buy the cheapest things as a default action. Many inexpensive appliances will actually cost you way more in electricity. Energy saving alternatives seem more expensive at first, but they will make up for that after they save you a whole lot of power.

Repair and replacements are also more frequent when you buy cheap goods. Think about how much money you are really going to save, before you go for the absolute cheapest option. By spending

<Save Money on a Low Income>

just a little extra, you can often get an appliance that is much better.

Keep Your Car Maintained

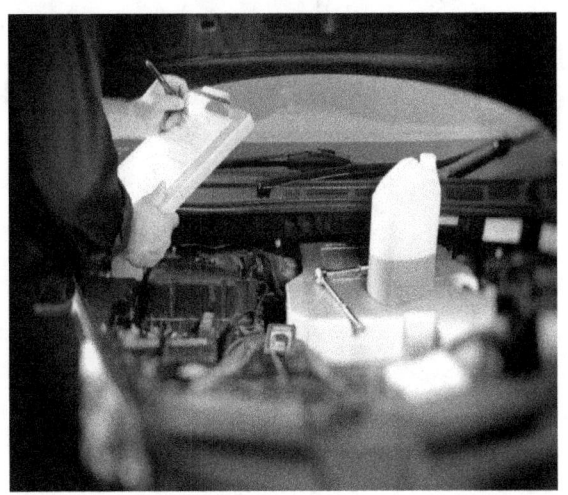

You might think that you are saving money, by neglecting to get your car serviced on a regular basis. A car that is not running optimally tends to use more gas, oil, and other consumables. In addition, there is a much higher chance that your vehicle will break down in the future. Suddenly, instead of having to cover the cost of a service — you will be stuck with an expensive, unexpected bill for parts and repair.

If you need your car, don't be a cheapskate by never getting it serviced. That kind of thinking will come back to bite you later. When you do pay for car parts, don't just ask for the cheapest ones available. They are more likely to break sooner, and then you will be stuck buying the same parts again.

<Save Money on a Low Income>

Why Not Do-It-Yourself?

Hand Crafted Gifts

Gift giving is a wonderful way to show people that you care about them. Of course, it certainly isn't very kind on your bank account. People have come to expect store bought items these days, but they might be pleasantly surprised to receive something that you created yourself.

There are plenty of ideas for gifts that you can make, even if you are not the crafty type. How about some quality candles, instead of the chemical filled ones that you can purchase. If you are handy in the kitchen, you can make delicious baked goods, or other tasty snacks.

As well as being cheap to make, your unique gifts will make people feel special, knowing how much time and effort you spent on them.

Learn to Cook

Cooking is good for more than just saving money on takeaway food and pre-packaged meals. It can become a wonderful hobby as well. If you are busy in the kitchen, creating all manner of delectable foods, you won't be out spending your money on other things.

Learning how to cook can drastically reduce your costs. Think of every item that you buy, and work out if it would be cheaper to make it from scratch. Home-

<Save Money on a Low Income>

made food always tastes better, and contains more nutrients.

Cook in Batches

While you are making your own food, think about cooking in big batches. Instead of just making a single serve for each person in your home, put together enough for several meals. You can store them in the freezer, using airtight containers. When meal times next comes around, you won't need to worry about cooking a thing. Just heat up those meals, and take some time to relax.

Cooking in batches is also a nice way to use less electricity or gas in the kitchen. Why have the stove on for an hour to make just one dinner? You could be sorting out food for half the week for the same price.

Try Making Things

In addition to cooking and baking, you might want to try your hand at making other things. Do you need a new bookcase or table? You might find a cheap and flimsy item for sale, but how about making something sturdy instead? When you build your own furniture, you can wind up with something of very high quality, without spending much money.

It's hard to beat the sense of pride and satisfaction that comes from building something with your own two hands. It can also turn into a great hobby, or even a way to earn extra money by selling what you make.

If you're not much of a carpenter, think about the many different items that you might be able to make. Try knitting or sewing your own clothes, or making arts and crafts to decorate your home. People used to do that sort of thing all the time, instead of rushing to the store to buy everything.

Increasing Your Income

The ultimate goal of this book is to show people that there are many ways to save money, even when confined by a minimal

<Save Money on a Low Income>

income. However, struggling is always going to be part of your life, unless you are earning enough money to be comfortable. For most people, that means earning more. While that's not the focus of this book, here are a few tips to give you some ideas and motivation, of that's your goal.

Use Free Money Offers

Are you eligible for government assistance? You will never know if you don't go and find out. Many people who are on low incomes are able to get supplementary payments to help them get by. Even if you're unable to receive any money, you might be able to get help paying for certain goods and services, like rent or medication.

Some people are too proud to ask for assistance, and that is their own decision to make. If you really want to start saving, maybe it's time to accept a little help. There's no shame in that.

Find a Second Income Stream

"Of course", you are probably thinking. "All I need is more money!" Well, maybe this idea seems too obvious to be useful, but give it a try. Now is the best time in history to start working for yourself on the side. The Internet has opened up new careers for people all over the world. You can sell your services, or goods, to people from any state, or even other countries.

Maybe earning more money isn't as hard as you think. You just need to find something you're good at, and give it a try.

Take Classes

Why would you choose to take a class, especially one that costs money? If you ever want to increase your income, so that you can save more, improving your skills is like a golden ticket. After you have some new qualifications, you might be able to get a better job. Maybe your employer would be willing to cover the cost of some classes, so that you can do

<Save Money on a Low Income>

your current job better. It might even end with you landing a nice promotion.

Never assume that you can't improve your career prospects. No one is going to just hand you a better job though. You need to have the right skills to pay those bills.

CONCLUSION

You now know plenty of ways to save money, even if you are barely getting by. There is no excuse for not having any savings. All it takes is the right decisions, some careful planning — and the strength to actually follow through.

You can save money on a low income. Good luck!

www.ingramcontent.com/pod-product-compliance
Lightning Source LLC
Chambersburg PA
CBHW070230210526
45168CB00019B/1225